He[Mr. Ross

by Maggie Fitzgerald
illustrated by Brett Colquhoun

Harcourt
SCHOOL PUBLISHERS

Printed in the United States of America

ISBN 10: 0-15-351253-9
ISBN 13: 978-0-15-351253-7

Ordering Options
ISBN 10: 0-15-351211-3 (Grade 1 Advanced Collection)
ISBN 13: 978-0-15-351211-7 (Grade 1 Advanced Collection)
ISBN 10: 0-15-358021-6 (package of 5)
ISBN 13: 978-0-15-358021-5 (package of 5)

3 4 5 6 7 8 9 10   179   15 14 13 12 11 10 09 08

"I have a bad back,"
Mr. Ross says.
"We can help you,"
says Dora.
"We can do tasks for you."

2

"I can water the strawberry
plants," she says.
"This is my task."

"Here is Mr. Ross's van,"
says Dad.
"This is my task."

4

"This is not the best task!"
says Jade.
"Dora, do you want to help
me?"

"I don't want her task! I like the plants!" says Dora.

"Yes," says Dad.

"Go down the line and water them all."

6

"Here is a new task, Dora," says Mr. Ross.

"Thank you for helping me,"
he says.
"Now have some strawberries."